Beginners Guide to Fishing

written by Roy Briggs

Contents

Introduction

This book has a two-fold purpose. It is principally intended to help the beginner to a extraordinary Sport, whilst it is hoped that the more experienced Angler will find something to interest him, even if only to recall memories of some of his past successes and failures.

Angling is the Sport which makes everyone equal; one could not mention any walk of life, a representative of which is not encountered, at the waterside, in the great brotherhood of Angling. The river's bank knows no social status; the humblest may share the day's sport with the highest in the land-with companionship *and* the chances of success being absolutely equal.

This Sport too, takes us into the pleasant places of the land, where peace reigns supreme and where we are at one with Nature. Daily worries are forgotten, whilst we watch our float quietly waterborne by a patch of weeds, whilst we confidently await the bite of a fish.

Our minds may be occupied in deciding how we shall put our tackle round the side of that bush without getting in a tangle in the branches. Further, we may be debating in our minds where the next fishing holiday shall be spent. Whatever kind of fishing we are doing, the result is the same, *and we are relaxed and absorbed in our sport*. It is almost possible to forget one's name and address, whilst trying to entice a wily fish into taking the bait.

To the beginner, and even to many experienced Anglers, our earnest request is especially to read, mark and learn the chapter on "the Angler's responsibility". The beginner may have the best intentions in the world to carry out what he has read in this respect until he arrives at the waterside, where he may even see experienced Anglers throwing back fish into the water instead of returning them carefully. He wonders why he has been recommended not to leave litter on the bank, when he sees some even among the veteran Anglers leaving untidiness behind when they finish the day's fishing.

A USEFUL TIP!

A small circular celluloid tube approximately 4 ins. long by It ins. wide is affixed to the cast about 1 ft. 6 ins. above the hook and just above the ledger lead, on a fined length of nylon. After the hook has been baited, this tube is packed tight with damp Groundbait.

When the line is cast out the bait, tube etc., will sink to the bottom and it is claimed the ground bait thus used, gets into the right spot and gradually spreads itself over the river bed and gives good results.

When ledgering a small split cork is lightly attached to the line near the rod tip, and this cork is tied to the rod rest on about t yard of thin string or line.

The weight of this cork is sufficient to cause the line to sag a little whereby a bite is more noticeable. When the fish is struck and being played the cork falls from the line and being attached to the rod rest is not lost.

1.   Baits and Groundbaits

The above items constitute a most important part of an Angler's outfit. Groundbait, as its name implies, is for use on the "ground", which, in this case is the bed of the river or lake, wherein one is fishing. Its main object is to attract fish "into the swim", i.e. into the area where the Angler will have his baited hook.

The place for the groundbait being on the bottom, it stands to reason that it will have to be made of such a consistency that it will sink, and this consistency is governed by the type and the state of the water being fished. The Angler has no need these days to go to the trouble of making up bread or bran in special forms, when Groundbait is so easily obtained at all good-class Tackle Stores.

In still water, Groundbait should be slightly damped and thrown out in a fairly loose mass, so that on striking the water it breaks up and sinks slowly down in little feathery clouds. It is this cloudiness which is attractive to the fish and it will be seen from afar in clear water. The nature of is such that it does not make a meal for the fish. In very slow-running water the cloud is very effective and, as is sinks slowly down whilst being carried along by the current, it will settle to the bottom in the form of a long "carpet". It is on this carpet that the Angler should have baited his hook can be used in a stiffer consistency as required for fast water. It is sometimes necessary to place a small stone in the centre of the groundbait, before throwing it out, when the water is very fast. This ensures its coming to rest within the limits of the swim. In very fast water it is often necessary to throw the groundbait well upstream, above where the Angler is sitting, in order to be sure of it coming to rest in the desired spot.

It is a, help in really heavy water to hold the groundbait in the hand, placing the hand under the water and then release, allowing the ball to roll to the bottom. This prevents the surface swirl from starting the breaking-up process.

It is advisable at all times to mix a little of the hook bait with the ground bait so as to encourage the fish to feed on that particular bait at the time of fishing. Samples of this should also be thrown out loose and in addition to the Groundbait.

Some Anglers prepare their Groundbait at home but others prefer to take along the bag of good ground bait as it comes from the Tackle Shop and moisten it up on the river bank to the consistency as required.

Most ground bait is put up in very convenient packages for carrying in one's bag or basket and the container serves for mixing and using on the bank.

Hook baits for fish are almost legion in number and variety. The favourite bait for Roach in one water may be useless in another or even in the same at a different time of the year. It is safe to say that all baits have their uses under varying conditions of weather, district and water. To give the beginner an idea of what he may use the list below will be of interest;

Used as Baits arc the following among many, Bread crust, Bread paste, Maggots, Worms, Elderberries, Hempseed, Macaroni, Wasp grubs, Caddis grubs, Wheat, Pearl Barley, Caterpillars, Earwigs, Wood-lice, Snails, Cheese, Bacon-rind, Potato, Grasshoppers, Bluebottles and Cherries.

Coloured baits are often very useful and the Angler should not hesitate to try them out from time to time.

For example, a green maggot is very killing on many and when one is fishing in the vicinity of bushes.

Worms are useful bait at times and all species of fish can be taken with them but they must be fresh and lively. To keep them so, they must be kept in some damp moss through which they can creep to keep themselves lively and clean.

Hempseed, wheat and pearl barley all have to be stewed before use. Unless they are to be fished in a water *which is known to surrender fish to these baits,* the Angler may have to fish a number of times before the fish get used to taking them. It is a case of experiment and perseverance. Samples should be thrown into the swim from time to time but not in handfuls. These baits are very filling and the fish will not feed to their own discomfort, so use the baits sparingly; half a dozen grains at a time being quite sufficient.

Elderberries are seasonable bait but at times they may be taken "out of season". They can be preserved in a formalin solution but must be very well washed before use, as the taste of this preservative is highly obnoxious to the fish. Failure to remove all traces of formalin is a sure way of keeping one's landing-net nice and dry-in other words-NO fish.

The beginner should always remember that, whatever bait he uses, he must include a little of this with his Groundbait when he feeds the swim. A most important factor is the size of the hook which is used. The beginner will probably read a lot about the correct size of hook with which to fish. There are two schools of thought on this subject, one says "small hooks" and the other says "large hooks". Both catch fish, so it is open to debate as to which it shall be. After many years of fishing experience, the writer has come to the conclusion that the small hooks hold better and also that it is not necessary to go below size 16 or above size 12. The latter is the larger. Match fisherman; however, go much smaller than the sixteen, but that is a different matter which will be dealt with later in this Book.

2.   Let's talk about tackle

There is an old saying which goes "One can judge a workman by his tools" and it applies in many ways to the Angler. It is agreed that many fish, and good ones too, are caught on what may appear to be seedy-looking tackle.

In these days there are an infinite variety of rods and tackle available from all tackle shops, from the cheap outfit for the young beginner to the elaborate and very expensive equipment of the specialist.

Generally it is accepted that the ideal rod for the average Angler, for bottom fishing is 10t feet in length, which will be found to answer in most types of water.

When an Angler goes out to fish, he should be as reasonably sure as is possible that every item of his gear is in perfect order. There should be no fear in his mind that the tackle will not hold a big fish. It has often been said when a good fish has been lost, that there must have been a fault in the line but very often the trouble is caused through a worn rod-ring. Continual casting and recovery of the line will eventually *cut a groove in the ring;* if there happens to be a kink in the line when a fish is being played, and this kink jams in the groove of the worn ring, a break is bound to be the result.

It is false economy to try and file out the groove in a worn ring, as the file will put in other small grooves, small, but nevertheless a starting point, at which the line can begin to cut in, when it will lead to a broken line. The *whipping* of the rod-rings: that is, the silk with which they are bound on to the rod, should be inspected for wear from time to time, as if it becomes rotted and a ring breaks away, *it is sure to happen when a fish is on the hook.*

Ferrules, (the metal tubes fitted at the ends of the rod joints) should be kept clean, well greased and free from dirt and grit. The use of stoppers is recommended to protect the ends.

Reels are expensive items these days and it is policy to keep them well cleaned and to give them an occasional oiling, using a fine oil. From time to time the bearings should be checked for any sign of play and he is a wise man who returns his reel to the maker occasionally for a general overhaul. Compared with the price of a new reel the charge for this service is small and can be considered as money well spent. Incidentally, a thread line reel is recommended for light tackle in use on a large lake, whereas on a narrow water such as a stream or canal a hook length; thus one gets away with the least loss of tackle.

Landing nets and keep-nets are next to be considered, and these should be watched for holes and rotting cord. Both these nets should be on the large side and the keep-net should also be deep so as to be well down in the water when fish are in it. The keep-net takes a lot of drying out and usually has to be packed wet at the end of the day's fishing.

Another useful item is a made-up cast carrier, complete with hooks and already shotted in various weights. This is described as a "Make-it-Yourself" job later in the book.

Never be afraid to scrap any hooks or casts showing signs of wear. Rod rests should be covered with rubber or plastic in the fork, to avoid any damage to the rod. Damp will creep into any break should the varnish on the rod be chipped. The rod should be thoroughly dry for storage and should be wiped well before being placed it its bag which in turn is hung up rather than stood in a corner.

A seat and tackle bag are necessary and such sundry items as knife, scissors, disgorger, spare casts, bait tins, etc., must be included.

Time spent in checking over one's tackle is never wasted and will save a lot of unnecessary expense. centre-pin does the job.

3.　Knots for nylon line

In the following images are illustrated knots. Careful attention should be paid to each stage, if satisfactory results are to be obtained.

THE DOUBLE THREE-FOLD BLOOD KNOT

1. Place the two ends, A and B, to be joined alongside each other as shown.

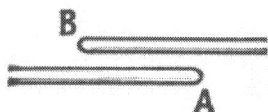

2. Twist the end 13 three times round the shaft of A, then pass B through the space formed where the ends just cross.

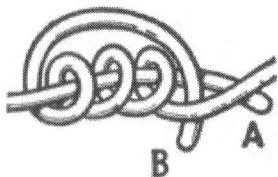

3. Twist the end A three times round the shaft of B, then pass A, in the opposite direction to 13, through the space formed where the ends just cross.

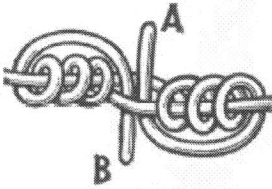

4. Pull knob tight and cut off ends A and B- unless you want to attach a dropper, in which case one end can be left long.

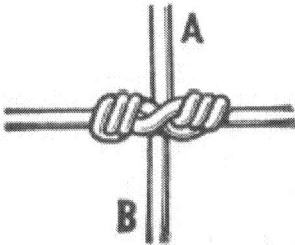

THE BLOOD BIGHT KNOT

1. Bend end of cast back 011 itself to form loop A.

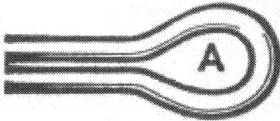

2. Twist loop A round cast shown to form loop B

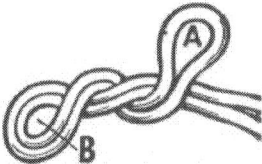

3. Pass loop A through loop B.

4. Pull knot tight and cut off free end,

THE TWO CIRCLE TURLE KNOT

1. Thread hook or fly, and slide up cast out of the way. Make first circle 6 to 8 inches from the point; overlay the second circle.

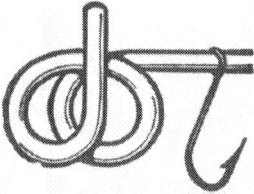

2. Holding the circles with the thumb and forefinger, tie a slip knot as shown. Tighten the slip knot and push the end of the line and then the hook or fly, through the two circles.

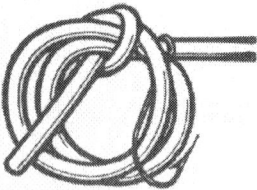

3. Pull on standing part, and circles-close one after the other. See that circles close round neck of hook or fly.

THE DOMHOF KNOT

1. This is an excellent knot for all types of hook. Lay a bend along shank of hook. Whip 8 turns along bend and pass free end A through loop of bend on last turn.

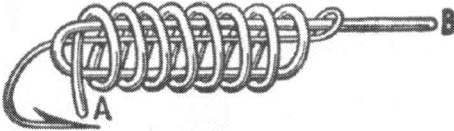

2. Pull knot tight. Where hook is fitted with eyelet pass line through eyelet before making bend.

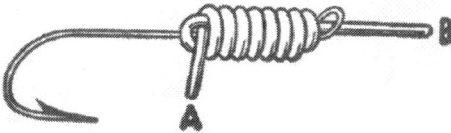

THE TUCKED SHEET BEND

1. Pass line A through, over and under the cast loop as shown.

2. Pass line A under itself to form a loop B.

3. Pass line A over itself and through loop B.

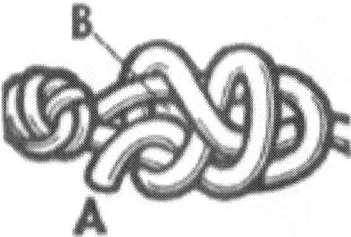

4 Pull line A tight holding its other end.

THE TWO LOOPS

1. If a loop is whipped on to the end of a line and a loop Is made on the end of a cast the two loops may be attached by passing the line-loop through the cast-loop and then threading the cast, point first, through the line-loop.

2. Pull on line and cast until knot is tight.

THE FOUR-TURN HALF BLOOD KNOT

1. Thread the end through the eye of the swivel and twist four times round the shaft.

2. Pass the end through the loop next to the eye.

3. Pull up tight and cut off free end.

THE DOUBLE OVERHAND LOOP KNOT

1. Bend end of cast back on itself to form loop A.

2. Twist loop A round cast as shown to form loop B.

3. Twist loop A round cast once more as shown.

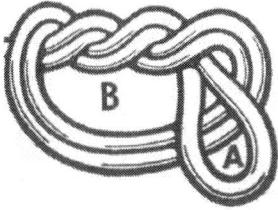

4. Pull knot tight and cut off free end,

4.   Balanced tackle

The above title covers a very controversial subject. It is not merely concerned with the balance of the rod and reel but with the complete outfit. A great deal depends on the person handling the tackle and what may be too heavy for one, might quite easily, be too light for another. It would be misleading to suggest any particular set-up with regard to this subject, because Anglers differ so much in their choice of tackle for the same purpose. What is of great importance is the balance of the weighted cast and float. This is the part which mostly concerns the fish and THEY don't get wed to tackle at any time. Fish are often termed "hook shy", but a better term would be tackle-shy.

One does not see an Angler using a Pike float with light roach tackle attached, but some do seem to try and emulate such a set-up. The cast should not merely be weighted to suit the float (although this is essential), but the weighted cast and float should be suited to the conditions of the water. That is, balanced to the current and suitable for the kind of fish being sought.

For instance, the Angler would not fish with a weighted float and cast without weight, in a whirlpool when in search of Barbel-but that method would be ideal when after Dace.

In coarse fishing, we usually go down to the bottom to get the bigger fish of the species such as Bream, Tench, Roach and Barbel.

Carp, Dace, Chub and Rudd, can be taken at varying depths between the surface and the bottom. Barbel are equipped with four barbules on the lower jaw with which they search the bed of the river for their food. These barbules are very sensitive and if a coarse line is felt, of which they are suspicious, they will not take the bait.

One of the basic principles is that the cast must be weighted, so as to prevent the fish feeling the weight when it takes the hook. In fishing *still water,* this is very important and cannot be stressed too much. One small shot is often sufficient to get the hook down to the fish and with such a tackle the Angler will only need a very small float. What of a lake which is shallow for some distance out however? In such a case extra weight will be needed to reach water of a fishable depth. This will require a larger float, which serves a two-fold purpose. It carries the extra weight required, whilst still maintaining tackle balance and it is easier to see at the greater distance. It is not always necessary to add more weight to the cast to carry the larger float. The alternative is to use a weighted float. When fishing in still (or slow-flowing) water, the Angler should err on the light side in his choice of cast. He should remember that if the tackle is moving at all, it will be very, very slowly. In addition, this type of water is usually very clear which gives the fish ample opportunity to inspect the bait before taking hold of it. If anything arouses their suspicion they will turn away and take the rest of the shoal with them. One has a better chance in running water because the fish have to be quick, lest another fish grabs the bait or the current carries it away from them. When the tackle is balanced with the shot on the bottom and with the float nicely "cocked", it is obvious that the weight, which is actually suspended, is sufficient to balance the outfit.

There are many ways of shooting a cast and most Anglers put their faith in their own ideas. Put briefly, the float should always be large enough to carry the amount of shot required and no more. If too light it will not hold up the tackle in the water; if too heavy it will offer too much resistance to the fish when the bait is taken.

When shooting for running water, the speed of the current must be taken into consideration. *It is better to string that shot along the cast,* rather than to bunch it all together. This is easier to find by practice than to explain on paper. Even the Novice will soon find out by observing the action of his tackle in the water. There are various types of weights-split-shot, half-moons and lead wire. The writer prefers split-shot, as they offer less surface to water drag.

The float is an important item and should be considered when one is making up tackles. Some Anglers change their float, but not the weight, hoping this will answer, but it is, to say the least, careless fishing. A float will do a specific job; it has very little latitude and one should not go beyond that point. Some interesting experiments on the shot-carrying capacity of any particular float can be carried out in a water butt or a bath full of water, where the results can be easily seen. This will provide the Angler with a lot of valuable information.

The beginner should remember that baits such as large worms have a definite weight of their own which should be taken into consideration when the casts are being weighted. In "ledgering", a large lead is used and this should be large enough to prevent the fish from lifting it up. It is a mistake to ledger too lightly unless in still water.

Whilst the writer is all for light tackle, it is a different proposition when ledgering. When the Angler intends to ledger he should cast well beyond the spot where he intends the baited hook to lie. The reason for this is' that the ledger lead must not splash into the water directly over the spot where one intends to fish. The fixed-spool reel has done away with a lot of ledgering, owing to the fact that light float tackle can be cast long distances by its use.

5.   Coarse fishing

Anglers everywhere impatiently await the "glorious 16th", that magic day when they will be able once again to sally forth to their favourite fishing spot. Hope runs high that perhaps this Season, they will get a fish which will set up a new record! The fish have finished spawning but in many cases are not fully recovered from this domestic effort. To regain their strength, the fish make their way to the faster waters of the river at this time of the year. Here they find more oxygen, which is a great help to them to recover their condition.

When you go fishing go to a good spot to fish is a weir-pool or the shallower runs of the river. In a lake, there is no such place so the fish will often gather in the vicinity of the mouths of feeder streams where they can feel the effect of whatever current may be available to them.

Let us take a trip on a typical June day. We are up and away at dawn; the air is fresh and the birds are singing to herald what has every appearance of being a perfect day. Arriving in the country, we walk down the little lane to the stream, passing on the way the Keeper's cottage, where a wisp of smoke is just beginning to curl lazily upwards from the chimney. The water is at a nice level with a steady flow coming over the sill of the weir into the pool below. To-day we are out to give a novice friend his first practical lesson and we begin by teaching him to stand well back from the water's edge whilst he assembles his tackle. Also we see that he puts a bag of Groundbait into the water to soak, in readiness for feeding the swim. We hope for Roach to-day and we have brought along a nice selection of baits with which to tempt the fish. Everything is in readiness to start, so we open the bag of groundbait and a small handful is thrown in at the edge of a gentle eddy alongside some bushes. This is followed immediately by the hook baited with the chosen bait.

We watch the float being carried round the eddy and we are soon able to anticipate its course and drop in a few samples of the selected bait ahead of the line it is taking. We expect these to reach the bottom about the time the baited hook arrives at the spot. The float goes slowly round and round with the hook just dragging along the bottom. A little more ground bait is thrown into the swim and almost at once the float goes down and the line streaks across the pool. No doubt about this, the fish is well hooked and feels to be a good one.

The novice handles the rod in the manner in which it has been explained to him and we find we have had a very apt pupil, who has taken in all that he has been told.

In a few minutes the fish is brought to the side and the landing-net is slipped under him. The first fish of the season, a nice Roach of about 12 ounces, and not at all bad for the first attempt! So the day goes on and quite a few good fish follow the first one to the net.

When it is time to pack up and make for home, the fish in the keep-net are *carefully* returned alive to the water, despite the fact that our novice would rather like to take one or two home just to prove his prowess.

The sun is setting behind the trees, with every promise of a fine day on the morrow!

FISHING FOR THE VARIOUS SPECIES

Rather than take them in alphabetical order we will start with the most prolific, most sought-after fish of all our freshwater fish...

1. THE ROACH

The roach is the most popular of them all and is so widely distributed to be found in waters varying from the small wayside pond and tiny stream to our largest lakes and rivers. Roach can be taken at various depths but the best fish are always on the bottom. A look at their mouths will show that the upper lip protrudes over the bottom one which indicates turning the mouth down when they open it to take food. For this reason the best method is to fish with the bait on the bottom either by laying-on or with the tackle travelling along with the current. This may well lead to fewer fish but they are larger. Groundbait is essential, particularly on a well-fished river.

Groundbait is all that is required. If maggots are being used, a few should be thrown in from time to time, using the ground bait merely as an attractor to bring the fish into the swim. Roach are fish which like the company of their fellows, so, having got one, you can be sure there will be more about.

2. THE BREAM

Bream are fish of the warmer months of the year although it is sometimes possible to catch them in winter when the days are not too cold and if one is fishing in deep water. A very pleasant evening can be spent sitting by a quiet lakeside waiting for one's float to go under to the pull of a big Bream. Although these fish grow to a large size, the old idea of using heavy tackle is fast being superseded by light lines and small hooks with the result that better fish are caught. These fish usually inhabit still or sluggish water, so the tackle should be fine-for "they have all day" in which leisurely to inspect the baited hook; if their suspicions are aroused they will not take the bait. The Angler should start, as in Roach fishing by getting out a sprinkling of ground bait round the area he intends to fish. This feeding should not be too heavy and here again, samples of the hook bait should also be thrown in.

The baited hook should lie well on the bottom for Bream and one should not be in a hurry to strike, as the fish are very used to taking their time over things.

If the fish are biting shy, a size 16 hook with a very tiny bait will often bring them to feed. It is also wise to get the tackle out near a weed bed when these are about. All fish are to be found in such places, as weed beds provide shade from the sun and sanctuary from their enemies, in addition to providing a source of food supply in the shape of the small water insects and snails which abound therein.

Bream do not put up a terrific fight when hooked, but their steady pulling and boring can be nerve wracking to the beginner. He should refuse to be beaten and should play the fish gently, when after a few minutes struggling, all being well it should be in the landing net !

It is often possible to see a small string of bubbles coming to the surface of the water and moving along at the same time. In a Bream water, this is often a sign that the fish are searching in the mud on the bottom for food. The Angler should note the track and will take fish from the shoal by casting ahead of their route.

This can go on until the fish take fright for some reason or cease to feed.

A look at the illustrations of fish and you will see that the Bream is a deep-bodied fish and will appreciate that to take a bait off the bottom it has to stand almost on its head. On coming back to an even keel, it lifts the whole of the tackle and we get the characteristic

Bream bite. The effect of lifting the tackle clear of the bottom, including the shot on the cast, the float tends to 'judder' over backwards.

3. TENCH

Here again we have a branch of the sport which is devoted to the warmer months of the year. These fish do not feed much in winter unless there is a long mild spell, when they may come forth for an hour or so in the middle of the day. Slow-flowing and still water is the home of Tench and they are not found either in fast water or in water which flows over a gravelly bed. The fish love to root about in the mud on the bottom and it is here that the bait must lie.

Carp waters often contain Tench as both fish thrive under the same conditions. Although the latter fish are unpredictable feeders at times, they are not so difficult to catch as Carp and one is not kept waiting long hours for a bite. With regard to baits for Tench, the list once again is a long one. In some districts, green peas are said to be a good bait, although some experts having tried them many times, and in various waters, cannot claim any success with them. Worms, maggots and paste are good and it is necessary to use groundbait to attract the fish to the swim. In the search for Tench, Groundbait will once again be most useful.

It is a wise plan to feed up a swim, near a patch of weeds-and to land the fish as best one can. It is sometimes useful to allow a little slack line if the fish makes for the weeds when first hooked. This often causes them to turn away, thinking that they are free.

When hooked, Tench have not the dash of a Roach but they have a way of using their broad fins in an effort to escape and on fine tackle they will give the Angler some exciting sport. When the float begins to "bob" do not be in too much hurry to "strike", but wait until the fish begins to move the float, well under or across the water.

4. CARP

A glance at the rod-caught Records will give an idea as to the size which Carp attain. In spite of this however, the Angler is still exhorted to use fine tackle which, of course, must be strong. Carp are found chiefly in still water and moreover, in water where weeds abound.

When Carp fishing, one must be prepared to lose some tackle. The Angler cannot go casually to a water and take out big Carp just off-hand! It is necessary to choose a likely swim and to persevere in the place, to feed it and to keep one's self out of sight of the fish. A lot has been written on Carp fishing and doubtless a lot more could still be written without coming to the end of the subject. In the main however, intelligence plus a knowledge of the habits of Carp will go a long way towards getting amongst these monsters. Patience too plays a large part, as can be seen when one reads of the time waiting for a bite by the habitual Carp fisher in his efforts to get a specimen fish.

There is a great variety of baits and methods by which one can try to take these fish. A lot depends on the water, as will be appreciated. A favourite bait on one water may not be of much use on another. It is not essential to cast the tackle a long distance out from the bank as the fish very often cruise round the edge when feeding.

When the bait is taken and the fish feels the pull of the line it will make for the nearest weed bed. If it is a big fish the Angler will have his work cut out to prevent it reaching sanctuary. Before the fish is hooked, however, there are a few things the Angler should know. It is useless to keep drawing in the bait to see that it is alright. Carp take a long time to make up their minds and if the bait is pulled away from them, they will take fright and refuse to feed. There is no point in being dogmatic as to the position of the bait, for Carp will take bait from the surface as readily as from the bottom. One thing is certain and that is that the tackle must not be too obvious to the fish or there will be no bites.

A good method, if circumstances allow, is to cast out beyond the weed beds and then let your line rest on a lily leaf, drawing it in until the bait is just under the surface at the edge of the leaf. Carp are fond of taking food, in the form of grubs from the underside of these leaves and they may well take your bait if it is in a similar position.

Carp-fishing is essentially a summer sport; the fish appear to hibernate in the winter, though on very mild days towards the end of the season the Angler may be favoured with a bite. The Lakes on country estates are likely spots to fish for Carp. It takes a long time to "grow" a good Carp water and these estate lakes have usually been in existence for a long time.

The many aspects of Carp fishing could occupy a lengthy volume, but a few "do's" and "don'ts" may prove helpful:

DO let your bait stay in one position and do the same yourself.

DO return your fish carefully to the water.

DON'T stamp about on the bank (This applies to all fishing no matter what species you are after).

DON'T get your baits tainted from your hands.

DON'T get the idea that your bait may have fallen off when it hit the water.

DON'T think that you require shark tackle because the record fish is such a good weight. You are more likely to meet up with 4-pounders than forty four.

DON'T panic when you feel your fish. They are not always as big as you think. A 1 ½ lb. Carp is capable of towing a boat containing two people for quite a distance.

Although many of the difficulties of Carp fishing have been briefly mentioned it is not with the intention of scaring the Novice, but just to show what to expect.

Once one has caught a heavy Carp, he will want to go for them again and again.

5. DACE

The Dace is a sporting little fish which provides the Angler with some fine thrills if he uses the lightest tackle.

The fish can be taken on a variety of baits including most small insects and paste. Being a small fish the tackle should be light with a small hook and a smallish bait.

The Angler should search the faster runs for Dace and he need not fish on the bottom as the fish will take the bait at all depths. When groundbait is used it should be in the form of a cloud and here again ground bait fills the bill to perfection. When fishing a deepish swim, the cast should be made up with the smallest shot nearest the hook so that the current can lift the bait up and down which enables the Angler to cover the water at all depths. The vagaries of the current will lift the lightly shotted cast upwards and where the stream eases, the bait will fall lower in the water again.

This movement is very attractive to Dace, which are rather partial to a moving bait.

The Angler should cast a few samples of whatever bait he is using into the swim from time to time, to keep the fish on the alert. Dace are very fast-biting fish and the Novice will do well if he can hook one fish in seven, until he gets used to their ways. A rod-rest is useless when Dace fishing, as there is not the time in which to pick up the rod when the float goes down.

Plastic maggots are ideal for Dace fishing. They save a great deal of time, as this bait does not have to be renewed at every bite, and Dace will bite every time you swim your bait downstream.

6. CHUB

Now we come to a very worthy opponent and he who would catch Chub must tread very warily indeed. Of all the fish to be found in British waters, the Chub is the shyest of the lot. I have known beginners who have, at times, almost given up hope of ever getting one at all! They provide good sport all the year round and like the Perch, provide the Angler with a roving day.

When in search of Chub, one does NOT sit in the same spot all day long, taking fish after fish. The Angler is indeed lucky if he can take two or three from one shoal without the remainder becoming scared. Caution is the keynote and the Angler has literally to stalk his fish and must be able to fish and control a fairly long line. One cannot take Chub when fishing with the hook under the rod top,

These fish are known for their diverse tastes in the matter of baits and, at times, they like a fairly large mouthful. A live Minnow is readily taken at the beginning of the season. He will also take an artificial one when the mood is on him. A small frog does not come' amiss at times. Amongst other baits we have worms, paste, cheese paste, macaroni, cherries, banana cubes, bread crust, various live insects and artificial flies. There are probably many more things which would be taken by Chub but the foregoing list will show that the changes can be rung almost indefinitely.

When hooked, Chub know the nearest way to all the snags in the river bed and the Angler cannot call the fish his own until it is in the net.

One must look to the rivers and streams when in search of Chub, although they have been introduced into one or two lakes with a certain amount of success.

The fish are usually found in small shoals and are fond of lying under bushes where they can wait for any of the grubs which fall from the leaves. The Angler should keep well back from the bank, because any shadow falling on the water will scare the fish away, *as will any tremor caused by heavy footfalls.*

Chub feed at all depths, from the surface to the bottom, and can take a bait easily from any position. The baited hook follows in the track of the ground bait and the game is on. The tackle should be allowed to travel down the swim at the same speed as the current; The Angler should occasionally hold back the line for a second to make sure that the hook is travelling in advance of the rest of the tackle. When the fish takes the bait, it will make straight for the bottom; the Angler should tighten the line and be prepared for squalls. The lips of this fish are very tough and once the hook has a good hold it is rarely that it pulls out.

In winter, the Angler should search the deeper water under the bank where there are bushes. One should cast well upstream in Chub-fishing, so that the tackle has a chance to straighten itself out before reaching the spot where the fish are expected to be lying.

7. RUDD

The Rudd is a sporting fish and, like the Chub, can be fished for with all kinds of bait from artificial flies to worms. Unlike the Chub however, it is a fish which favours still or slow-flowing waters and appears to thrive well under these conditions. The Norfolk Broads district is a stronghold of these fish. It is often necessary to fish a long line for Rudd; they are fond of taking a bait which is fished just under the surface.

Rudd will fight in a manner very similar to that of the Roach and light tackle is recommended if the best sport is to be enjoyed. A size 14 hook is about right for the largest of these fish. Summer and autumn are the best times to fish for Rudd for in winter they tend to keep out of sight. Fishing from a boat is a popular method when searching for Rudd, but the novice should be very careful if he uses this method.

Rowing over the area is fatal to success. When using a boat, the Angler should let it drift the last few yards and the anchor should be lowered into the water without a splash. The float should be small and the cast should be very lightly shotted. It is a good plan at times to fish with an unshotted cast so that the bait sinks slowly and naturally in the water and is more attractive to the fish.

8. BARBEL
When the trees are beginning to change colour and there is a freshness in the air which denotes the approach of autumn, the Angler can well try his hand at Barbel fishing. In this Fish, one has a worthy antagonist; the fight put up in the waters of a weir- pool is something that will not be forgotten after having once been experienced.

Baits for these fish are varied. At one time thousands of lobworms would be thrown into a swim a few days before attempting to fish. Barbel are such fickle feeders that *even then* the fishing day would turn out to be a complete failure. What may *appear* to be a good day for Barbel may turn out poor and vice versa. Heavy tackle is not much use even though the fish run to big weights. If the fish see or feel the cast they will refuse to feed. Never the less, the tackle must be strong, as the fish are very often in fast and heavy water and weak tackle will not hold them in such places.

The groundbait must be made to a fairly stiff consistency in order to get it to the bottom quickly in the fast water and it should also carry a liberal sample of the hook bait with it. It is best to your ground bait at the water-side, i.e. when one has seen in what state the river is running. The novice should appreciate that ground bait must not on this occasion be used as a cloud or it will be carried out of the swim before it has sunk above a few inches in the water. It must be made up stiffly!

Worms are regarded as the bait *par excellence* for these fish, using a size 12 hook. When hooked, the fish keeps on the bottom as long as he possibly can; at this stage the Angler must not exert too much pressure or the fish will "stay put." It is better to give a little slack line in the early stages of the fight, in an attempt to delude the fish into thinking that he is free. When he moves off, the Angler should tighten and attempt to keep the fish away from the bottom.

A Barbel does not fight near the surface until he is almost tired out and so when the fish has been seen the landing-net should be made ready.

9. PIKE

When the first frosts of winter are experienced, the Pike Angler begins to think of his sport. There are two ways of catching Pike-spinning and live-baiting.

The former method is the most sporting but it often happens that a Pike may be disturbing a Roach swim and the Angler will then resort to the use of a live-bait in order not to disturb the Roach. When spinning, the

Angler uses artificial baits or lures of all kinds including spoons, minnows, plugs, etc.

The art of spinning is not too difficult to acquire and the novice should go along with a friend for half an hour so as to get the idea of casting and retrieving the lure. The recovery of the line is a most important factor, as the lure down below performs in accordance with the actions of the Angler on the bank. A good method is to spin the lure nearer the surface on a mild day in clear water and near the bottom in very cold weather or when the water is highly coloured. The reason for this is that in clear water a lure that is fished high can be seen by the Pike from a greater distance. In coloured water the lure is not so easily seen, so it is fished near the bottom where the Pike will be lying.

Hook points should be kept sharp as Pike have very bony mouths which are difficult to penetrate. Pike fight well when hooked on light tackle and the novice should not try to haul the fish to the net or gaff too quickly or a break will be the result. It is safe to say that the average weight of Pike is five or six pounds with a few running to double figures being caught each year.

It will be apparent therefore that very heavy tackle is not required and if the Angler should hook one of the monsters it is all the more to his credit if he manages to land it on the fine tackle.

It used to be that the bigger fish were always taken on live-bait and the larger quantities of fish on spinning tackle. With the advent of the present-day light tackle however it is interesting to note that big fish are now falling to spinning lures.

The paternoster tackle is very good for use in weedy water before the weeds have died away. It prevents the live-bait seeking refuge in the weeds and is a definite advantage in the right type of water. Paternoster tackle is easily made up at home and this is explained in the chapter "Make-it-Yourself". There is no need to use heavy tackle when live-baiting nor is it necessary to cast out to long distances, as Pike very often lie quite close to the bank. Here again the

Angler should rely more on his skill in playing the fish than in the strength of his tackle and in his apprenticeship days every fish lost should be counted as a lesson learnt and the mistakes not to be repeated in the future.

If one is fishing in a lake, the bait should be in the vicinity of a weed bed or near the trees on the bank, as the fish lie in these places waiting for their prey, but great care should be taken to keep a hooked Pike from rushing into the weed bed or he may be lost.

Another method used for Pike is fishing a dead bait on the bottom of ledger tackle. This is proving to be a good method of taking big fish and very often the bait used is a Herring, proving that the taste of sea does not come averse to the Pike. Dead fish are used for fishing what is known as the sink-and-draw method, which consists of putting a fish on a tackle which carries a weighted spike. This is pushed down the mouth of the fish with the hooks along its side. The bait is dropped into the water where it dives head first towards the bottom. It is then pulled towards the top so that the motions it described in the water are very similar to those of an injured fish.

Bleak or Gudgeon are ideal for this purpose and the small sea fish known as Whitebait are also good.

However, one of the most important things when fishing with either live or dead-bait is the use of groundbait.

Ground Bait will do the job, used as a cloud in still water, not too heavy, as it will tend to hide the bait, particularly if it is suspended a foot or two off the bottom.

10. PERCH

What Angler cannot recall his first attempts at fishing and the first fish caught. This would most likely be a small Perch, as these fish are bold biters. Small Perch are indeed very obliging sometimes to the youngster fishing with his bent pin on a stick! They are a different proposition when they grow bigger and wiser.

A big Perch will give the Angler a run for his money at any time and a Perch on the hook is by no means a Perch in the net. Like Roach, Perch are fond of company and are found in shoals except when they are very large and then they will be alone or perhaps in pairs. Tackle should not be heavy but it should be strong. This statement has been repeated many times in this book but its importance cannot be over-stressed.

Perch are well distributed and are found in all types of water from the large rivers to the small ponds, gravel pits and lakes. A river Perch is a beautiful sight and he fights far better than his brother of the lake. The Angler should fish at mid-water when searching for these fish and a lively minnow or worm is a good bait or, if the Angler prefers he can spin for them. In fact, a

Perch is often taken on the lure intended for a Pike and this also applies when one is using a live-bait.

Serious ground baiting is done when one is Perch fishing, but as with Pike, a small sprinkling of ground bait will encourage Minnows and suchlike to the swim.

As Perch feed on these, the latter will follow the small fish when they want to feed. A Perch of about a pound in weight and caught in a clean river is not to be despised as an item of food for the Angler-and many people prefer them to Trout.

11. GRAYLING

This fish is more of a game-fish than a coarse variety, although it is a member of the latter family. It is closely related to the Trout, is found in the same waters as Trout and can be taken on fly tackle. It actually provides sport to the Trout-fisherman after the Trout season has come to a close. In many districts however, it is fished for with the same baits as are used for Roach etc. and on float tackle.

Grayling like to lie at the tail-end of deep pools and they come up in a swift glide to take their food.

Unlike Trout, they are not put down easily by bad casting. Grayling fishing will teach the novice more about tightening the line, in preference to a decided strike, than other kinds of fishing: the reason for this is that Grayling have very tender mouths and if one makes a hard strike, the hook will be pulled away and the fish will be lost.

Unfortunately when this happens, the fish often leaves part of its lip on the hook, which means there's a damaged fish in the water, prone to disease, which can spread to all the fish in the river.

It is folly to try and hurry a hooked Grayling. When the first light frosts come, the Grayling are in good condition to be fished for and they will give sport right through to the end of the season. It is better to fish the swim for these fish and the cast can be shotted as described for Dace so that the bait fishes the water at varying depths. It is good practice to fish a long line and light tackle throughout is the order of the day!

6. The protection of our fishing

In addition to the care of tackle and the careful handling of the fish when caught, there is one aspect of our fishing which needs far more care and attention than anything else connected with angling. That is, the water wherein we catch our fish. Of late years, the increase in the number of Anglers has been colossal and with this increase, there is a decrease in the amount of water available for each Angler. In addition to this, there is the problem of areas of water being closed to Anglers.

Many miles of canal have been closed or filled in and this has led to the loss of valuable fishing which has affected thousands of Anglers. This has forced the unfortunate ones to travel to other waters which have now become too crowded and many clubs have stopped the issue of day tickets in consequence.

The 1939 War was responsible for many Factories being built in the country in the UK, out of the way of bombing.

Waters which had been crystal clear became polluted and the fish died. In spite of the Law against pollution, this calamity often happens and although Fines are imposed, they do not bring the waters back to their previous condition. It may be years before such a place is worth fishing again and the Anglers who visited it are perforce compelled to go to other places, which latter may perhaps be over-fished already.

A great many Angling Clubs contribute yearly to some sort of charity or society that looks after the purity of the water. One might pause to think for a moment on one's chances of going fishing at all, in a few years time, if nothing is done to maintain and improve the waters that are available to us to-day.

7.   On organising a fishing holiday

To the really keen Angler, there is no better prospect than a fishing holiday to be spent either at a favourite spot or in visiting new scenes. One most important point which must be stressed is that it is useless to be haphazard in making the arrangements. It is so easy to be thorough in the matter, that it isn't worth the risk of neglecting any point which goes to make such a holiday worthwhile.

There are various ways of spending a fishing holiday in so far as accommodation is concerned: camping, staying at a farmhouse or country cottage, living in a caravan sited near to a good water, a holiday afloat or if the Angler requires the finer comforts of life, at a good Hotel. Whichever is chosen, there are certain factors common to all.

Camping is now very popular and in this connection food becomes one of the chief items to consider. It is very nice to wake up early in the morning and emerge from one's tent to admire the peaceful lake in its sylvan setting. It is also very nice to anticipate a freshly caught Perch to go in with the bacon-but let the novice bear in mind that a Perch every morning may get a bit monotonous before the holiday is over. Regarding the actual camping, if one is going to a favourite spot perhaps visited each year, it is necessary.

to make sure that the place has not changed hands and that the water is still available for fishing. A water may have been taken over by a Club and made private since the last visit. Arrangements should also be made with the landowner to ensure that all is in order for pitching the tent, so that there is no "slip-up" at the last minute.

The tent should, of course, be pitched in a spot where it is not liable to become waterlogged in the event of rain. If the site chosen is farmland, the camper should make some arrangements with the farmer for the supply of milk, etc. Sleeping arrangements are also important and the novice should bear in mind that *it can be very cold near the water*, so that ample equipment in the form of blankets, sweaters or pullovers, etc. should be taken.

It is worthwhile including a good sleeping bag in one's kit. One should not camp too near the water's edge, particularly if it is a river. A sudden rise in the level may flood everything out. Remember, too, that it does not need to have rained where you are for this to happen

There may be a cloudburst up in the hills, of which one. may be unaware, but it may bring the water over the bank in very quick time during the night. The ideal spot then, is on rising ground a little way from the water's edge, preferably near a hedge, which will afford a certain amount of shelter.

Staying at a farm or country cottage can be very pleasant and a lot of the difficulties of camping, such as food preparation, cooking and washing up are overcome.

There is no feeling that the time when one is cooking a meal is just the time that the best fish are on the feed! However, whether Farmhouse or Hotel, there is one thing to be remembered and that is-meal times are as arranged.

These places have to be run to a routine and, although their arrangements MAY be somewhat elastic, it is wrong to expect to be able to stretch this too far. One should also make sure that the selected accommodation caters for

Anglers and by this we really mean "caters for Anglers" and not just accept them! One should know whether the Hotel is prepared to put up snacks and flasks to take out for the day and whether a meal will be available if the Angler should be a little late in the evening.

One should always enquire whether there are means of heating in one's bedroom. If the weather is cold, a little warmth is well appreciated! There should also be facilities for drying clothes, in case one gets caught in a sudden shower. Regarding the packing of snacks, the Angler should make sure as to how these are to be paid for and whether they are included with the weekly charge. A small thing but one which could cause a little unpleasantness when the time to settle the bill arrives! If the fishing water is some distance away, one needs to know all about transport facilities.

Caravan life has come to stay and we see more and more each season. There is not much that can be said that has not been included under Camping, as the two are closely related. If you hire a sited van, be sure that you are near enough to obtain provisions, etc, and if you are towing one behind your car, make sure of your site and its amenities before you book it.

A holiday afloat appeals to a multitude of people as no doubt many of us fancy ourselves as sailors. You may have boat knowledge but, if not, the hirers will soon put you wise to it. The Norfolk Broads usually are the first to come to mind for such holidays but there are countless miles of waterways in various parts of the country where boats are available for hire and where you can obtain excellent fishing.

As usual, ascertain the fishing facts first, then all the details about the boat, insurance of craft, moorings, etc. and provisions for the start of the trip. On the way you will be able to victual the boat at the various towns or villages through which you pass.

A good form of holiday is being in a boat if it is only a hundred yards off-shore, or, if the case of a lake or river, three or four feet from the bank. This gives that completely detached-from-it-all feeling which is half the thrill of fishing.

Having fixed up the fishing permits (and his accommodation) the Angler should make sure about his supply of baits and tackle. A visit to the nearest tackle shop, for local information, unless the water belongs to a Club, when a letter to the Secretary will bring all that you require to know. A few useful hints on actual fishing from a boat are given in Chapter Eight.

8.   Fishing from a boat

Boat fishing calls for a flat-bottomed punt to get the best results. It allows the Angler to move about a little bit without rocking in the water and setting up disturbances which are detrimental to successful fishing.

When hiring a boat, however, you have to take what is available so we will not go into details about the best boat for fishing. All we are concerned with is the handling of it and the procedure toward good fishing.

Before setting out from the side, you should have your tackle assembled and set out in the boat so that it is to hand, to avoid having to move about a lot once you have cast off from the bank.

Assume you are all set and afloat. Row out towards the spot you intend to fish and, as you approach it, ship the oars so that the boat will glide over the actual spot where your baited hook is to be. You should take a keep-net with a very small mesh which is for the purpose of your ground baiting, is put in the net which is hung over the side and shaken as your boat is gliding across. The net should be emptied quickly, as you do not want a trail leading up to the boat. Doing this has eliminated the problem of throwing groundbait out with its accompanying splash, which would scare the fish.

As your boat comes to a stop, lower the anchor or whatever form of hold you have, over the side without splashing and let it go gently to the bottom.

You can now begin to fish. There are a few hints about lake fishing from a boat. You should always have the boat anchored off a weed bed if possible. Fish in towards the weeds and from time to time throw some of the hook bait on to the weeds. Maggots or an odd worm will wriggle off the leaves and sink down in a natural manner.

Groundbait should be thrown in only at long intervals as the main offering has already been laid by means of the net. If you are using paste then from time to time throw a small pellet as near the weeds as possible remembering that paste cannot wriggle its way off.

If Perch are about you can fish with a worm at midwater where it will be more effective than lying on the bottom. However if the water holds Bream and Tench, the worm on the bottom may well be taken by one of these.

Be sure, by the way, that there is a baler in the boat, just in case. If in doubt about a sudden leak get to the shore as quickly as possible and beach the boat.

Finally, before leaving the boat, when you have finished fishing, make sure that there are no maggots or particles of groundbait left lying on the bottom.

Leave the boat as clean as you possibly can and ready for the next corner.

10. The fishing match

Our novice will now have probably joined an Angling Club and, attending the meetings he will hear about the fishing Matches which have been arranged for the Season. He will, no doubt, be wondering about the procedure on such occasions. When he enters his name for the Match, he must bear in mind that although he is a beginner there is no allowance made purely on account of its being his first venture into this side of the sport.

He is expected to have learned the basic things about fishing, particularly if it is a Club which specialises in Matches and in which the members go all out for the prizes.

The Rules for the Match are often read by the Secretary of the Club, immediately after the draw for places is over, and just prior to the contestants moving off to find their swims.

The novice goes along to find the peg bearing the same number as his draw ticket and on arrival there he will set up his tackle.

He must not wet a line until the starting signal has been given. In most Matches, he is not even allowed to put his groundbait in the water to soak until after the signal.

All his gear should be set out around him, so that he can reach anything he requires without having to keep getting up from his seat. This is not a rule, but it is done by the Angler in his own interests and to prevent scaring the fish. He himself may not mind having to keep getting up, *but the Anglers on either side of him may dislike him doing so.*

When the signal sounds, he should use his first swim down, as a means of checking the depth of the water.

The next job is to get the ground bait into the water and this should be done gently to avoid scaring the fish.

It is not advisable to fish under the point of the rod, as when a fish is hooked its antics may scare the rest of the shoal out of the swim. The best spot is about halfway along the swim and well above the next Angler.

The novice must not let his tackle encroach on the next Competitor's swim. The beginner must remember all he has learned about the ground bait *being* made to a consistency to suit the strength of the current.

Light tackle is the order of the day when Matchfishing and the Angler should not be afraid of going lighter than he does in ordinary fishing trips. Many good fish are landed by tackle which is almost as fine as a spider's web. If the novice does lose tackle and fish, he will nevertheless gain valuable experience which will stand him in good stead in future outings. He should go to his first match with the idea of learning; the possibility of winning taking second place in his thoughts. More than one kind of bait should be carried and if the fish "go off" during the Match, one should not hesitate to make a change of bait or tackle to suit the new conditions.

It is useless to look about, to see what the other fellows are doing, as this is the way to miss bites.-Many Anglers go "all out" for quantities of small fish and try to get sufficient to make up the top weight, relying on quantity rather than quality.

The novices should keep on trying all the time, however hopeless things may appear to be. If he doesn't get many fish he should blame himself first, the fish second and blame the swim last of all! Should the swim be impossible, he may lay a complaint to the banksman *but this must be done before the start of the Match.* Before making a complaint however, the Angler must try to make a fair judgement for himself and must not confuse a difficult position with one that is impossible. Not many of the latter places are pegged, as the men who peg the banks are chosen for their ability to do the job.

They do not peg swims which they would not be prepared to fish themselves.

Try to net your fish as quickly and quietly as possible and do not waste time admiring it. Get it into your keep-net and your tackle out into the water again quickly.

At the end of the Match a finishing signal will be sounded and then it is usual, if you have any fish, to stay at your peg until the stewards appointed to weigh them in have been along and done so. They will enter the weight on your card and in their book and you should see that these weights agree. After the weighing you should return your fish carefully to the water.

The beginner can help himself in Match-preparation when out on his fishing trips, by selecting what look like impossible swims rather than look for the easier places. There is a great deal of satisfaction in winning a Match which has been fished under difficult conditions- and particularly if the Winner is a newcomer to Match-fishing.

11. Make-it-yourself

As a spare time activity, particularly during the close season,
you may wish to try your hand at making some easy-to-
construct items of tackle.

The following hints may help to this end and give you some
useful equipment to use next season.

1. A Made-up Tackle Carrier

This little piece of equipment will be found to be one of the
most useful you have. On it you can carry as many as a dozen
made-up tackles of different weights.

For instance, have three, one carrying a dozen made up
tackles with size 12 hooks, the second the same number with
size 14 hooks and the third made up with size 16 hooks. Have
three different weights of shots so that you have four tackles
made up in three different hook sizes and this enables you to
change over in less than a minute and without having to
waste time making up a new cast while fishing.

The basic material required is a piece of wood or plastic. The
size is 5" X 4" and the material is one sixteenth of an inch thick.
Three, this size, fit nicely into a large tobacco box.

You also require a cork mat for making the two strips on
which to wind the tackle. A small round file about 1" is also
needed and with this you file the grooves along the top and
bottom edges of the material. Trim off any burr caused by the
filing as this could cut into your casts if left on.

Next cut two strips of cork the length of the material and, slightly roughening the place where they have to fit, cement them on with a waterproof cement, such as Durofix. Opposite each groove in the material you then cut a triangular groove in the cork strips. On the bottom strip you then slit the cork between the groove" and this slit, which is made with a razor blade, is used to take the end of the cast. The hook is stuck into the top edge of the top cork strip. This completes the Tackle Carrier and a dozen tackles can be accommodated on each one. Figure 1 shows the finished article.

2. A Simple-to-make-Spinner

This simple spinner, which can be cheaply made, is one which has been used for many years and it certainly takes Pike and Perch, in addition to being responsible for many sea fish coming to the net. The materials required are two medicine bottle corks, a piece of brass or copper one sixteenth of an inch thick, a couple of split rings which can be purchased in the tackle shops, a swivel and a treble hook. Also needed is a piece of Perspex for the vanes.

First of all cut the metal to be the same size as two half-corks which will be cemented on each side, plus a short length over at each end to allow a small hole to be drilled to take the split rings. The corks are then cut carefully lengthwise so that there are four halves. The metal should be rubbed over with coarse emery cloth or filed to roughen the surface, which then gives cement a better grip.

Smear one side of the metal with cement and the flat surface of two pieces of cork and place the corks on the metal with the broad ends meeting in the middle of the plate and the small ends tapering to each end of the plate, which will give the shape of the spinner. Next, place the remaining two pieces of cork on the other side and allow to dry. The two holes in the plate will have been drilled first of all.

When the cement is dry and the corks firmly fixed they can be rubbed down smooth and also the edge of the plate, which will now be sandwiched between the corks. When the job is smooth and looks neat, two slots can be cut, about half-way along one cork and repeated on the other side. The slots will take the spinning vanes which can be cut from the Perspex, or, if preferred, thin metal.

These can also be cemented in and the spinner is then ready for the hook and swivel. It can be painted to represent a fish or finished in, say, blue and silver.

By using larger corks you can make a set in various sizes. They are cheap enough so that there is no need to worry if a couple are lost on snags during a day's fishing.

3. An Easy-to-make Pike Float

Here is a float which, owing to its great buoyancy, will carry quite a large live bait. It can be made quite easily and cheaply and will last for years.

The materials are: a table-tennis ball, a six-inch length of dowelling about 1" diameter and a rod-ring. Ordinary sewing-cotton can be used to whip the ring to the dowelling.

Push a steel knitting-needle through the ball, getting the point exactly opposite, and push it through the other side. You can enlarge this hole if required, to take the dowel but the latter should be a tight fit so must be done carefully. Allow about three inches of the dowel to come clear at the end, which will be the top of the float. When you are satisfied about the position apply waterproof cement liberally all round the dowelling so that when set there will be a complete joint. If this is not done water will get in and the float will sink.

Next, whip on the rod-ring near the bottom, and your float is complete except for a piece of cycle valve tubing for the float cap and the top half of the ball painted red or orange.

4. Self-cocking Float

For this you require elderberry pith for the body and this is easily collected on one of your fishing trips. It should be taken from dead wood so that it is hard.

Cut a piece about 1 ½ inches in length, using pith of about 2" diameter and then push a knitting needle carefully through the centre of it and out at the other end.

Next take a piece of dowelling at one end, whip on a small hoop of copper wire. Now push the dowel through the pith until only the loop protrudes at one end. At the other end cut a piece of the pith carefully through all round and about 1" in length and remove this. Set it aside as it will be required later. Then push about five brass shoe nails into the bottom of the float all round the dowel and their position in the float. When these are in, take the cement and smear the bottom, which will be where the nail heads are, also one end of the small section previously cut off. This is then placed back on the dowel and allowed to set.

The end nearest the loop is tapered of l" with a razor blade to the general shape and it is then finished off with smooth glass paper all over. The top portion of the float can be painted to the colour preferred. A float cap is fitted on the end of the dowel and you now have a self-cocking float.

5. Paternoster Tackle

This is a simple piece of equipment to make and requires only a bubble float and a piece of Perspex as the main items.

The Perspex should be cut, and three holes drilled. It is suggested that you insert three eyelets, similar to those used in the lace holes of shoes. Arts and Crafts shops usually sell these and they should be obtained first and drill the holes of a size to suit.

The eyelets need to be a tight push fit but not so tight that they have to be forced in or they will split the Perspex when they are flattened down on the other side.

This flattening process should be carefully done.

The rest of the item is self-explanatory in the drawing, as all you need is a couple of swivels and a lead. The Perspex arm is far more effective if rubbed down with emery cloth to take off the shine, as it will not then flash in the water.

12. The angler's responsibility

Over the last few years there has been a great increase in the number of Anglers, which speaks eloquently of the popularity of the sport. As a body, Anglers are always pleased to welcome a newcomer but they often forget that they hold a great responsibility to these novices. Teach the beginner how to fish by all means, but teach him also the rules of the game. There are a number of experienced Anglers however, who, quite good at catching fish, often ignore the other side of the game.

We allude to the preservation of fish, the returning of fish alive to the water, the respecting of the rights-of-way to the river bank and many other similar details.

The possession of fishing tackle does not entitle you to fish where you please. It may be necessary to have a permit from the owner or the lessee of the fishing rights. This is usually in the form of a day ticket.

Nature can cope with her own problems, but she cannot take care of the Angler's depredations. One of the first things an Angler must learn is that he has the responsibility of helping to maintain the stock of fish in the waters where he enjoys his fishing. Failure to do this is the surest way of ruining the sporting value of the water. To overcome this, or rather to help in the maintaining of fish life, these things came into being the keep-net, the size limit and the quota of fish allowed to be taken away on anyone day.

It takes a fish two or three years to reach the size when it is of interest to the Angler and if each Angler took say, five fish from the water every day, the stock would very soon be depleted. The obvious thing is to return all fish alive to the water and (what is of even greater importance) to return them carefully and individually.

Throwing fish far out into the water causes injuries from which they often die, or injuries which cause disease and which they can spread, throughout the whole of the stock in the water. Fish *have* been thrown yards out into a lake or river, a keep-net *has* been emptied on the bank and the fish kicked back into the water-these things *have* been done by so called *Anglers*, of experience and who should have known better. *Such practices do not help in the preservation of our fishing.* Glass-cased fish are always regarded with mixed feelings by the thinking Angler. There is no point in laying fish out on the bank to gasp their lives away in torture, whilst the Angler poses beside them to have his photograph taken to show his friends what a good fisherman he is. How much bigger would they have grown had they been returned to the water and (what is more important) what fine producers of sturdy fish for the future of the sport?

Anglers themselves are the people who have the remedy in their own hands and it should not be necessary to have to enforce rules for the safe return of the fish to the water. Clubs are a great help in such matters but there are vast numbers of Anglers who are not club members and who fish waters where no such rules apply.

The least they can do is to guard their interests by handling every fish carefully. The youngster taking up fishing should be taught these things as carefully as he is taught to assemble his tackle in the correct manner.

We Anglers are indebted in many instances to landowners who allow us to fish the waters on their estates.

From time to time, we hear of water being closed to the Angler. The maintenance of an estate costs a great deal of money these days and it is up to the Angler to see that no damage is done on such lands. It is easy to put one's feet on a barbed wire fence to get into the next field and the first time or two may result in no damage but in time the wire becomes slack or broken and may allow valuable stock to go astray. No landowner is going to grant privileges and have to pay for repairs afterwards.

It may not seem much to "nip across" a field, but where there is even a vestige of a "track" *others will follow* and soon there is a wide path across the field. It may be a little further to walk round the hedgerow but it does show appreciation of the privileges granted.

When an Angler asks for permission to fish, he should also ask how he can reach the fishing without trespassing.

The owner will appreciate such an enquiry; he will know at once that here is an Angler who will do no wilful damage. Hinges are a useful invention and make gates easy to open! Some Anglers do not appear to know that by the same rule *they make the gates easy to close.* Litter is another offence; one piece of paper or a cigarette packet doesn't look very bad but think of the sight if a hundred

Anglers all leave such litter on the bank after a day's fishing. It is easy to dispense with an empty bait tin by throwing it in the water but it is no trouble to take it home with you in your tackle bag. Never on any account leave a bottle behind when packing up at the end of the day. Otherwise the usual mischievous boy comes along, breaks the bottle, with most dangerous results to the farmer's cattle or dogs. We know of one case where a valuable pedigree cow had to be destroyed, through injury due to lying on a jagged piece of bottle glass left by an Angler. Most Anglers realise all these things but the few who don't imperil the privileges enjoyed by all of us.

13. The end of the season

This little book, like the fishing season, must come to an end. The novice can look forward to many pleasant hours spent by the waterside. From his first step, he will be storing-up memories, which he may not think about for some time but time moves along and as he gets older, he will realise what a storehouse of recollections are in his mind and from which he can draw when, in turn, he talks to the youngsters who are coming up. What is the novice going to do until the "glorious16th" comes round again ~ In the three months, he can (if he wishes) fish for Trout or perhaps, if he lives near the coast, he may do a little sea fishing. If he doesn't wish to go out fishing, he can get books on the Sport from his Public Library and do a little "reading up". He should also get the books dealing with the life-cycle of underwater insects. This knowledge will be of help to him in his fishing later on. During his first Season, he will have gained a lot of experience and he may have half-formed ideas of what to do this time when that time comes round again. If he is of a mechanical turn of mind he may decide to make a few items of tackle for himself-here Chapter

Eleven will be helpful-and when future fish are caught with these he will feel doubly proud of his achievements.

He may feel the desire to try his hand at rod-building and if so, he will purchase a building kit and do the job.

It is not very difficult, as the timber is already shaped and it is a most interesting experience.

One thing the novice should do. He should look back on his first Season to find out if he has done any of the things he should not have done. He should make a resolution to play the game better during the coming Season.

He should have kept an Angling Log-book for himself showing how this can be set out. It is useful in giving him information, at a later date, regarding how the fishing has gone under certain conditions. He will see which places fish best at certain times of the year. It will recall incidents of the day in question, as he glances through its pages.

We close the Chapter and end this Book, by wishing Anglers everywhere "tight lines" and some real rod benders. To the beginner: don't forget that *someone* has to catch the big fish! Set about your fishing carefully and correctly *and it may well be you.* Play the game ALL the time and just as you were helped in the beginning, in turn don't refuse help to another. We all have to learn and whilst we can find out a lot from our own experiences, a little advice "upon the road" is never to be despised-and should not be denied.

14. Glossary of angling terms

Bait - This name is given to any insect or substance which is put on the hook for the purpose of catching fish.

Bait Dispenser - A device, attached to the line, filled with ground bait and lowered into the water when it automatically opens and drops the 'feed' to the bottom.

Baiting a Swim - The act of putting Groundbait into the water as a means of attracting fish to the spot where the Angler intends to have the baited hook.

Baiting Needle - A type of needle used for threading hook-link through a bait, such as a piece of potato or a small dead fish, for use as a spinning lure.

Bottom Fishing - The term applied to angling with float or ledger tackle. Refers to Coarse Fishing as opposed to fly-fishing or spinning.

Butt Cap - The metal cap at the bottom of the cork grip on a rod.

Butt Joint - The bottom joint of the rod.

Butt Ring - The bottom ring of the rod.

Cast - A length of line or Nylon placed between the line and the hook-length and on which the weight used to get the tackle to the bottom is placed. This should be rather weaker than the line and stronger than the hook length.

Casting - The art or action of throwing out the baited tackle into the water.

Close Season - The period of the year when it is illegal deliberately to fish for any species of coarse fish. Some Authorities allow small fish to be taken for the purpose of using them as live-bait for Pike, where the latter fish are allowed to be taken. The Close Season, which naturally represents the breeding period, is from 15th March to 15th June, both days inclusive, but there are slight variations in some districts.

Coarse Fish - The name given to any freshwater fish other than Salmon, Trout and Sea-Trout. The coarse fish family consists of Barbel, Bleak, Bream, Carp, Chub, Dace, Eels, Grayling, Gudgeon, Perch, Pike, Roach, Rudd, Tench and the smaller fish, such as Minnows.

Disgorger - A small instrument forked or notched at one end, used for removing the hook from the mouth of a fish, when the bait has been taken too far down to allow the Angler to reach it with his fingers.

Flight - The trace, or cast, used when spinning. It may be made of Nylon or fine wire.

Float - The name given to the item of tackle which suspends the cast in the water and registers the bite of a fish. Floats are made from variety of material and in numerous shaped or styles.

Gaff - A pointed instrument in the form of a large hook, screwed or whipped to a handle. It is used for getting large fish out of the water when a landing-net would be useless.

Gag - An implement used for keeping open the jaws of pike or other large fish while the Angler extracts the hooks without danger to his hands.

Gentles - A bait used by coarse fishermen. It is the grub of the blue-bottle.

Groundbait - Used for the purpose of "feeding a swim" in order to attract fish to the spot. It should be soaked in water at the river bank. The state of the water is a deciding factor as to the consistency at which the groundbait shall be used.

Hook Length - This is the length of line or Nylon to which the hook is bound. This should be about twelve inches in length and always finer than the cast.

Keep-net - A net of fine mesh, with a wide mouth, in which fish caught are kept alive until the end of the day. It is suspended in the water while the Angler is fishing. The larger the Keep-net, the better.

Landing-net - This net is used for lifting the fish from the water to land them. Landing nets are fixed to a metal frame which, in turn, is mounted on a handle. It should be good-sized and used in preference to a gaff whenever possible, as it does not damage the fish.

Laying-on - This is a type of ledgering practised when one wishes the bait to remain stationary. It is used, as a rule, with a float and split-shot on the line, and in some districts is known as float-ledgering. A deadly method of taking fish.

Leads - The lead is the weight used to get the baited hook to the bottom and is made in various forms such as splitshot, which is a small shot cut halfway through, the cast being placed
in the groove and the split closed up with a pair of pliers. Half-moon leads are small flat leads which are easily folded on to the cast and can be quickly removed when necessary

Ledgering - This is a form of fishing in which no float is used. It calls for the use of a heavy lead which is placed on the cast and rests on a small shot, in order to allow the line to run easily through the lead when a fish takes the bait. It is used a lot by night fisherman and also in river fishing, when there is a strong stream running. When fishing in "still" water, use ledger leads as small as possible-even to the size of a pea.

Line-float - A type of grease which is used for dressing the line to make it float on the surface of the water.

Link-swivel - A useful attachment where a swivel is fixed to the line and cast is quickly looped on or removed when tackle has to be changed. It is used for attaching a flight or trace to the line and is chiefly used when the Angler is spinning.

Live-baiting - A form of Pike-fishing in which a small live fish is used, mounted on
a snap tackle and cast out into the water. This form of fishing is losing its popularity and spinning or the use of dead bait is replacing it.

Lures - Artificial forms of bait which include spoons, plugs, imitation fish, live or dead natural fish according to the species being fished for.

Minnows (Artificial) - These are imitation fish used for taking Pike and Perch when one is spinning. They are made in a variety of materials, including soft plastic which feel more natural when a fish takes hold.

Minnows (Natural) - Small fish which serve as a good bait for Perch and often taken by Pike; Chub will take them early in the season. They can be preserved in formalin for use as dead baits for spinning.

Paternoster - A piece of equipment used for bottom fishing in weedy waters, or for taking Perch bait, ensuring that the bait does not bury itself in the weeds.

Plastic Baits - These are realistically made and a worthy addition to the Angler's tackle bag. At present they are made in the following forms: worms, maggots, chrysalis, tadpoles and caterpillars.

Plugs - This is the name given to certain lures which "wobble and dive" rather than spin in the water and are used for catching Pike or Perch. Many are made of wood and are suitable for fishing weedy waters, as they do not sink if the Angler stops recovering line for any reason. They are made in many sizes and types.

Plummet - A small pear-shaped lead, which is used for finding the depth of the water. The hook is put through the ring at the top and then the point is inserted into the strip of cork which is found at the bottom. The float is adjusted so that it is just above the water level.

Rod Fittings - Rings-These are placed at intervals along the rod and carry the line, so that a gentle curve is given to the rod when a fish is on. They are made in a variety of styles. The top ring and also the butt ring should be lined with Agatine or Porcelain in order that the line can run with the minimum of friction.

Ferrules-These are the metal pieces which are fitted on the ends of the joints so that the rod can be assembled. They should be protected by stoppers when not in use and kept free from dirt and grit.

Grip-This is the handle and is made of cork. It should be lengthy.

Reel Fittings-These are the two rings which slide on the cork grip and "position" the reel. Screw Reel Fittings can now be obtained and these ensure that the reel cannot work loose, as can happen with ordinary slide rings.

Rod Rests - Can be purchased or easily made by the Angler and consist of a forked piece of wood or metal. The rod is placed in the fork whilst waiting for a bite. The fork should be rubber or plastic covered to protect the rod.

Snap Tackle - An assembly of two treble hooks on a short length of wire which is used for attaching a small live fish when live-baiting for Pike or Perch.

Spade End Hook - A form of hook which has become popular and consists of a flattened top shank in the form of a spade. Anglers tie the line or Nylon to these and the spade prevents it slipping off.

Spinning - The art of bringing a lure through the water in imitation of a small natural fish. This is a method of taking Pike and Perch, especially in winter. One form is known as a "Devon Minnow" and the vanes on the body cause it to spin as it is drawn through the water.

Spoon - A form of artificial lure used in spinning.

Striking - The art of lifting the rod-to drive home the hook point when a fish has taken the bait. The novice should not think the term denotes the use of great strength; a gentle flick of the wrist being all that is called for.

Swim - The strength of water along which the Angler is allowing his tackle to travel.

Swimming the Stream - The practice of letting the tackle be carried along by the current, with the baited hook just clear of the bottom.

Trace - line or wire to which lure is attached when spinning or live-baiting.